C000214357

CUNARD QUEENS

Conceived, designed and produced by

Open Agency
Mill House
8 Mill Street
London SE1 2BA
www.openthebook.com
+44 (0)20 7740 7000

Written by **Elspeth Wills**

First published 2011
© Open Agency Limited
All images © Cunard Line & Open Agency
Apart from page 44 © Ian Murray
and page 143 © Paul Macleod

978-0-9542451-9-1

Printed in China.

CUNARD QUEENS

The story of the six Cunard Line Queens

*'Queen Victoria truly epitomises
the new golden age of ocean travel.'*

Peter Shanks, President, Cunard Line

CROSSING TO CRUISING

For the first time in history six Queens have reigned over the Atlantic within a century.

In July, 1840 Samuel Cunard's Britannia made the first regular mail run between Britain and North America. Comfort came second to safety and speed. Early passenger, Charles Dickens, found the cook drunk, the cabins leaky, the berths as narrow as coffins and the Saloon like a gigantic hearse.

Over the decades the fleet grew and the time taken to cross fell from weeks to days. Cunard was a record breaker not only in speed but in comfort including the first nursery, gym, smoking room and passenger suites at sea.

By 1914 Mauretania, Lusitania and Aquitania were the largest, fastest and most sumptuous liners on the North Atlantic. Then came 'the war to end all wars'. In 1915 a U-boat torpedoed the Lusitania with the loss of over 1200 lives: many smaller Cunarders serving as troop carriers were also sunk.

By 1925 with the flagship Berengaria, formerly the German liner Imperator, and eight new passenger ships, the fleet was buoyant once more. The next year Cunard announced a bold move - two super-liners rather than three ships to provide the express shuttle between Southampton and New York. These were the first two Queens, Mary and Elizabeth.

It was a hugely risky venture. The ships were built during a decade of falling passenger numbers, depression, a forced merger with White Star and increasing threat of war.

Although Queen Mary made her triumphant arrival in New York in 1936, Queen Elizabeth's maiden voyage was a very different affair as, half-finished, she was secretly moved to New York for safety. After years of ferrying troops and then war brides, both Queens underwent a major refit to replace graffiti and bunks stacked seven high, with grand pianos and potted palms.

The 1950s were the golden era of crossing. In 1957 Cunard enjoyed its most profitable year ever. Sea, however, was no longer 'the only way to cross': in the same year air overtook it in terms of passenger numbers. By 1960 jet setters were deserting the Queens, now seen as stuffy and staid.

Cunard shocked the world in 1959 with plans for a revolutionary design of liner which would cruise as well as cross. Critics saw the future Queen Elizabeth 2 (QE2) as a white elephant.

They were nearly proved right as the project suffered cancellation, delays, shipyard strikes and technical teething problems. After a stormy start in 1969, QE2 won the world's heart and became possibly the most popular Cunarder of all time.

Most people assumed that QE2 would be the last ocean liner. Again they were proved wrong. Forty years on, as the supersonic Concorde fleet was withdrawn, Queen Mary 2 was on the stocks and QE2 was still sailing. By now the US Carnival Corporation owned Cunard Line although they traded on Cunard's British heritage.

Queen Mary 2 broke all records of her day as the largest, longest, tallest, widest and most expensive passenger vessel ever built. She proved so successful that Queen Victoria and Queen Elizabeth followed hard on her heels. The new Queens marked the return to the elegance and luxury of ocean travel, but now available to more than the privileged few.

3 ELIZABETHS, 2 MARYS & 1 VICTORIA

Over the past 75 years the six Cunard Queens have commanded the seas, with a period of only a few months when there was no Queen in service.

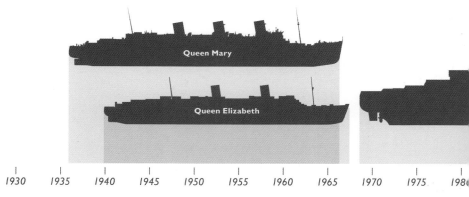

Queen Mary
1936-1967

Built during the Depression for the express Atlantic service. Served as a troop carrier helping win the Battle of the Atlantic. Resumed normal service in 1947 after ferrying war brides. Sold to Long Beach, California, as a museum and hotel.

Queen Elizabeth
1940-1968

Dashed secretly to New York on her maiden voyage. After 64 crossings as a troop ship began passenger service in 1946. Resorted to cruising from 1962. Burnt out in Hong Kong while being converted to a floating University.

Queen Elizabeth 2
1969-2008

Shocked the world by her modernity. Combined crossing with cruising. Served as a troop carrier during the Falklands War in 1982. By 1996 Cunard had invested more than 10 times its initial outlay on her. Sold to Dubai as a museum and resort.

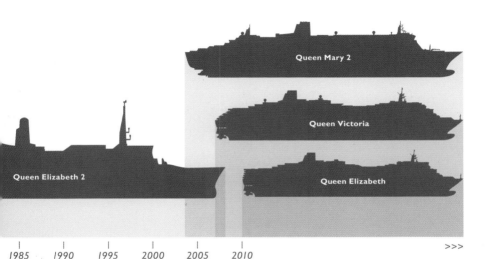

Queen Mary 2

Queen Victoria

Queen Elizabeth

Queen Elizabeth 2

1985   1990   1995   2000   2005   2010   >>>

Queen Mary 2
2004-

Largest ever transatlantic liner and the first since QE2. Flagship of Carnival Corporation's Cunard Line. Floating hotel during 2004 Olympics. First world cruise in 2007. Final meeting with QE2 in 2009. Rendezvous beside Statue of Liberty with younger sisters in 2011.

Queen Victoria
2007-

The smallest of the trio of new Queens and the first Queen not to carry mail. Undertook her maiden voyage to northern Europe before setting out on her first world cruise. First Cunarder to have a woman Captain at the helm.

Queen Elizabeth
2010-

The youngest Queen and the second largest Cunarder ever built. On her inaugural world cruise sailed close to where the first Queen Elizabeth sank in Hong Kong Harbour. In 2012 pays homage to her namesake in Southampton during the Queen's Diamond Jubilee.

CONTENTS

Artist at war
page 130

Buildi

'Human audacity in steel.'

Percy Bates, Chairman, Cunard

BLUEPRINT FOR A QUEEN

Two remarkable men designed six remarkable ships

Sir John Brown, designer of the first Queens, happened to share the same name as the shipyard which built them: 'I was just a wee laddie from Glasgow with the most famous name in Clydebank'. He joined John Brown's shipyard as an apprentice in 1919 and retired as Managing Director of John Brown's shipyard as QE2 was being planned.

Right Sir John Brown and shipyard sign.

'With Queen Mary 2 we re-wrote the rules of maritime design'.

Twelve year old Stephen Payne read in the 1972 Blue Peter Annual that 'The Queen Elizabeth was the last of a great age - nothing like her will ever be built again.' The statement moved him to write to the presenters of the Blue Peter television programme, putting forward his ideas for a future super-liner.

Above Stephen Payne alongside his story featured in the Cunardia exhibition on board Queen Victoria.

Blue Peter wrote back, politely dismissing them and enclosing a Blue Peter badge. In 2004 the architect of Queen Mary 2 was invited to appear on the programme. This time Stephen received a gold Blue Peter badge. He is now Chief Naval Architect for Carnival Corporate Shipbuilding.

Left 1972 Blue Peter Annual and the Blue Peter badge that Stephen received.

MADE TO ORDER

On winning an order, the first thing the shipyard does is to assign the future vessel a number. It is chalked on each piece of the jigsaw that makes up the ship.

Queen Mary

534

Watching the men pouring back through John Brown's gates after 27 months of enforced idleness, the local MP commented: 'These are the men who years later will tell their children "I worked on the 534." '

Queen Elizabeth

552

535 was the Cunarder that was never built. Confident of winning the contract, John Brown's reserved 535 for 534's sister.

Concerned that it looked like a fix, the British Government asked Brown's to change Queen Elizabeth's order number to 552.

Queen Elizabeth 2

736

736 was more often referred to as the
Q4 project: she was always going to be
a Queen. Her predecessor Q3 never left
the drawing board. Loss of passengers
to the airlines led Cunard to postpone
and then cancel the contract .

Queen Mary 2

G32

G32 was the order number chalked by
ALSTOM Chantiers de L'Atlantique on
the 300,000 parts that went to make up
Queen Mary 2. Her order number is now
the name of her night club.

Queen Victoria

6127

Work started on Queen Victoria as 6078.
Given the success of Queen Mary 2, Carnival
Corporation decided that 6078 was going
to be the P&O cruise ship Arcadia. A day
later, on 5 April, 2004 they unveiled the real
Queen Victoria, Fincantieri's order no 6127.

Queen Elizabeth

6187

Queen Elizabeth was the first Cunarder
built at Fincantieri's Monfalcone yard.
Over a hundred years old, Monfalcone
is the shipbuilder's youngest yard.

RIVETS TO ROBOTS

Shipbuilding techniques have changed dramatically over the last 75 years. Gone are the riveters scrambling like ants over the scaffolding of the first Queens. Now whole sections of the ship are prefabricated before being welded together. Robots have replaced many less skilled jobs.

Queen Mary

Gross tonnage	80,774
Dimensions (m)	297.2 × 36.1
Launched	1934
Build	Steel plates and 10 million rivets
Powered by	Steam
Constructed by	John Brown and Company, Clydebank, Scotland

Queen Elizabeth 2

Gross tonnage	70,327
Dimensions (m)	293.5 × 32.1
Launched	1967
Build	Edge-welded steel and aluminum plates
Powered by	Steam (diesel from 1986)
Constructed by	John Brown and Company/UCS, Clydebank, Scotland

Queen Victoria

Gross tonnage	90,000
Dimensions (m)	289.8 × 32.3
Floated out	2007
Build	Strengthened steel
Powered by	Six diesel engines
Constructed by	Fincantieri, Marghera shipyard, Italy

Queen Elizabeth

Gross tonnage	83,673
Dimensions (m)	300.9 × 36.1
Launched	1938
Build	Steel plates and 10 million rivets
Powered by	Steam
Constructed by	John Brown and Company, Clydebank, Scotland

Queen Mary 2

Gross tonnage	151,400
Dimensions (m)	345.0 × 41.0
Floated out	2003
Build	300,000 parts linked by 1000 miles of welding
Powered by	Diesel-electric and gas
Constructed by	ALSTOM/STX Europe, Saint-Nazaire, France

Queen Elizabeth

Gross tonnage	92,000
Dimensions (m)	294 × 32.3
Floated out	2010
Build	Strengthened steel
Powered by	Six diesel engines
Constructed by	Fincantieri, Monfalcone shipyard, Italy

Opposite, left column, top to bottom Queen Mary, Queen Elizabeth and Queen Elizabeth 2 in construction.

Opposite, right column, top to bottom Queen Mary 2, Queen Victoria and Queen Elizabeth in construction.

Gigantic, immense, colossal

The sheer size of the Queens almost defies imagination. Queen Mary was the largest, moveable, man-made object of her day and Queen Mary 2 is nearly twice as large. Comparisons helped the public think big and appreciate the craftsmanship that lay behind the sheer scale.

Each of Queen Mary's 35 ton screws were mounted so precisely that they could be turned by hand.

Queen Elizabeth was 50 feet taller than St Paul's cathedral.

Each of QE2's nine diesel electric engines is the size of a double-decker bus.

Queen Mary 2's engines produce the thrust to launch a Boeing 747.

Queen Victoria is just slim enough to fit into the Panama Canal.

Queen Elizabeth weighs over 7000 tons more than her namesake.

Above One of a series of 50 Churchman's cigarette cards designed to satisfy the public's insatiable appetite for information about the world's largest liner.

Opposite Driving in the first rivet, Queen Mary, 1930.

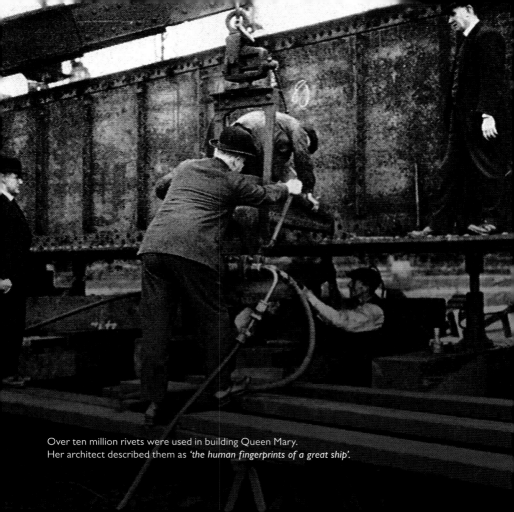

Over ten million rivets were used in building Queen Mary.
Her architect described them as *'the human fingerprints of a great ship'*.

'Listen to the snarl of steel on steel'

None of the first three Queens had an easy birth. Although Cunard talked of the snarl of steel in its 1931 Christmas magazine, another headline told a very different story: 'Clydebank workers face the worst Christmas for many years.'

The Depression halted work on 534 for 27 long months. Her rusting hull towered over Clydebank as a constant reminder of hardship to over 3000 unemployed shipyard workers. Seagulls nested on her cliff-like sides and starving cats roamed the yard.

A Government loan towards the two super-liners in return for Cunard merging with rival White Star meant that from Easter 1934 the town echoed to the sound of hammering once more.

Right Cunard Christmas Number Special 1931.

Opposite Queen Mary in construction at Clydebank.

... AND A TOILET SEAT

When Queen Elizabeth's hull was in the stocks from 1936, the order book at Brown's was bulging, Warships were the order of the day. When war was declared, bookings for her maiden voyage were cancelled.

The priority was to make her sufficiently seaworthy to move her from Britain, in line with Winston Churchill's instructions. Bombing such an iconic target would be a huge propaganda coup for Germany.

She had to wait until 1946 for the fittings appropriate to a Queen, from rare woods to silk wallpaper.

He just walked off the ship with the stuff

By the mid 1960s British shipbuilding was in terminal decline. Bitter industrial disputes, missed delivery dates and widespread pilfering plagued the building of QE2 and nearly bankrupted Cunard. Captain Arnott recalled: 'Some workers were stealing the ship faster than she could be built.'

The three younger Queens had much easier births.

Below An artist's impression of workers on Queen Elizabeth.

A toilet seat

A wall cabinet

Five lampshades

Four settee backs

Three lounge stools

Five sheets of plastic

180ft (55m) of fibreglass

Four wooden gratings

An electric radiator

Three bookcases

Four curtain rails

A bulkhead lamp

A shower valve

Two buckets

Two sheets

A drilling brace

A canvas tarpaulin

Eight gallons of paint

Thirty yards of carpet

Five fluorescent tubes

216yds (197m) of Sellotape

Two chests of drawers

350ft (107m) of cable

A roll of wire netting

Six table settings

Three cushions

Five curtains

A blanket

*Found in the possession of one QE2
shipyard worker when arrested in 1968.*

'Is my work hard? Yes, of course it's hard. But I wish they'd hurry up and give us another ship to build.'
Frank McCarron, Riveter

'Many of them do jobs that are useful but not much to look at. My work's pretty when it's finished.'
A. Gribben, Carpenter

'They call me rivet-boy, but my job's just as important as any of the others.'
Pat McKendrick, Rivet Boy

'I've fitted out more liners than you've got fingers - and fitted 'em out well, too.'
D. Vance, Fitter

'I heated so many rivets for her, I forget how many. They say there's ten million in the 534.'
Patrick Wood, Rivet Heater

'It's a pity she's finished, that's what I say. It's been a fine job to do and work worth doing.'
E. Blue, Fitter

'No. 534 was the first big job I've had. I hope there's plenty more like it.'
Robert Malcolm, Iron-Moulder

'Holder-on, that's me. What, not know what a holder-on is? Where did they bring you up.'
D. Chalmers, Holder-on

'My job was real work, putting in the boilers. They're some boilers, too, for a ship this size.'
E. R. Esplin, Boiler Shop

'It would suit me if they built a couple of Cunarders like this one every year.'
Alec Lowery, Machine Driller

'Rivet-heating's my job, too. How many have I put in? It would take a week to count 'em.'
George Row, Rivet Heater

'Yes, that's what I am, iron-moulder. My name's Malcolm. All iron-moulders are Malcolms.'
George Malcolm, Iron-Moulder

A NEW PEAK IN LUXURY AT SEA

Each Queen has adopted her own interpretation of a grand hotel at sea, depending on ideas of style, comfort and fashion of the era.

'She had a regal style, an elegance'

Queen Mary was the epitome of Art Deco at sea, competing with the chic of French Line's Ile de France. While most people loved the clean, sleek nautical lines, a few critics likened the ship to a cinema.

Although the Art Deco style celebrated 'the machine age', achieving it demanded impeccable craftsmanship to combine exotic materials and execute the painstaking detail. Artists, metal workers and carvers created the interiors of the 'Ship of Beautiful Woods' whose 56 species included cedar and satinwood. Not all the forty artists found favour. Cunard chairman Percy Bates demanded the removal of panels by Duncan Grant as unsuitable to his fashionable clients' taste. Bates' wife influenced him: 'We must have little deer and gazelles, you know.' rather than nudes.

'Here is revealed indeed the essential destiny of the Queen Mary to be lived in luxuriously but with good taste, in settings of exceptional splendour but without exaggeration … Spacious almost beyond belief, her hospitality is yet warm and intimate.'
'Queen Mary Cabin Class Deck Plan', 1936

'The keynote is solid comfort and snugness, characteristic of the best type of London or New York club, where deep leather armchairs in alcoves invite intimate conversations and a real coal fire blazes cheerfully in the grate.'
'Daily Telegraph', 1936, of Queen Mary's Smoking Room

Left Agnes Pinder-Davis was responsible for panels in private dining rooms, designed rugs and carpets, and chose many of the fabrics for Queen Mary.

Opposite Anna Zinkeisen was responsible for the painted screen on the starboard side of the ballroom on Queen Mary.

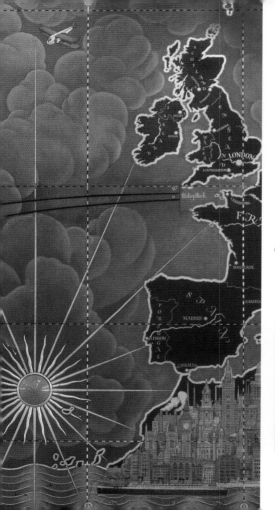

'The map depicts the North Atlantic ocean as connecting the New to the Old World. The ocean is only shown in blue along the ship's course, being dominated elsewhere by a cloudy stratosphere in warm shades of brown. A silver clock is placed high up in the centre, its numerals standing out in raised crystal, electrically lit. A crystal model of the "Queen Mary" electrically lit and synchronised with the ship in speed, steams across the ocean, through the nebulous stratosphere.'

Queen Mary launch booklet, 1936

Left Entering through bronze doors, up to 800 diners could be served at a sitting, in the largest public room at sea. No detail was too small: the rose pink upholstery of the chairs was chosen to show ladies' dresses to best advantage.

Left Queen Mary Cocktail Bar.
Right Queen Elizabeth Cocktail Bar.

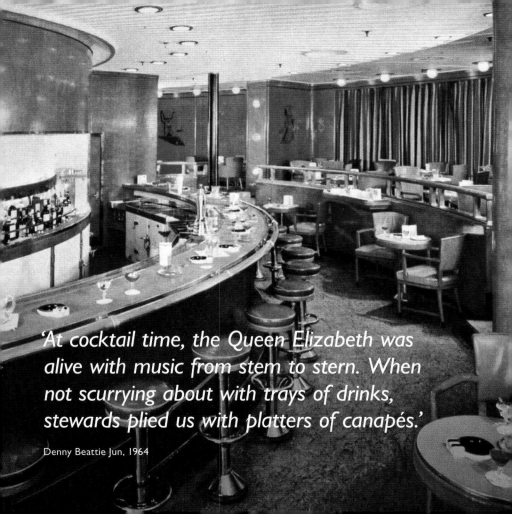

'At cocktail time, the Queen Elizabeth was alive with music from stem to stern. When not scurrying about with trays of drinks, stewards plied us with platters of canapés.'

Denny Beattie Jun, 1964

'Queen Elizabeth had a dashing style'

Queen Elizabeth was the first British liner to show her true colours after World War II. Style had moved on in the previous decade and Elizabeth was less Art Deco, more grand Elizabethan country house.

Not to be outdone by her elder sister, her interiors used 100 different tropical woods including a marquetry mural of the Canterbury Tales in the first class lounge. Even the Captain's cabin was panelled with wood, from the foundations of London's early 19th century Waterloo Bridge.

Above Queen Elizabeth's Cabin Class Lounge.

Opposite Margot Gilbert was one of several artists who worked on both Queens.

Below Queen Elizabeth Voyage book shows a variety of rooms on board, including the Main Lounge and Smoking Room.

'The pool itself is lined with golden quartzite, a stone used in the days of the Pharaohs. Seen through the seawater, it gives the impression of a sandy pool.'

'Queen Elizabeth Accommodation Plan', c1950

'*There's nothing of the old Lady about the new Queen Elizabeth 2. She is smart, crisp and modern.*'

'Daily Telegraph', 1968

'Something new and exciting for the holiday market'

Queen Elizabeth 2 was a radical departure from the past. Cunard hoped to shake off the image of 'aspidistra and public bar… dukes and duchesses and Knees up Mother Brown.'

QE2 was designed to attract the younger swinging set. According to the 'Daily Telegraph': 'a voyage on QE2 would become as much of a social must for the 'with-it' as a trip to Carnaby Street or the King's Road'. Princess Margaret, a leader of the style set approved: 'This new Cunarder will show that design in Britain is exciting and full of vigorous common sense - is always out in front, leading the field.'

'She's a swinging super-ship, controversially beautiful. She has a regal beauty all of her own. It's there for all to see, built into her smooth and simple, sleek and graceful lines. A ship surely to stir the hearts of a maritime nation.'

'Daily Mirror', 1968 of QE2

'We have designed the interior to look and feel like a ship; not something evocative of a hotel, another liner, or a baronial hall.'

Denis Lennon, joint head of interior design for QE2

A new look for the new Queens

The 21st century Queens blend the best of the traditional, from the Grand Lobby to the Promenade Deck, with interior design appropriate to the innovations introduced for ships dedicated purely to leisure.

Opposite Queen Victoria – First private theatre boxes at sea.
Below Queen Mary 2 – First planetarium at sea.
Above right Queen Mary 2 – First champagne bar at sea.
Below right Queen Victoria – First permanent museum at sea.

Making a grand entrance

The grand lobby has always been the focal point of a great liner – the place to meet, to see and be seen, to make a grand entrance down the sweep of the stairs.

The grandest of Queen Mary 2's five thousand stairs is the flight down to the Grand Lobby.

Queen Victoria's Grand Lobby was designed to combine the glamour of ocean travel with the luxury of a top class hotel.

An 18 ft high Art Deco marquetry frieze featuring the bow of the first Queen Elizabeth dominates the three-storey Grand Lobby of Queen Elizabeth. It was designed by Viscount Linley, the Queen's nephew.

Opposite Queen Victoria Grand Lobby.
Below left Queen Mary 2 Grand Lobby.
Below right Queen Elizabeth Grand Lobby.

THE ULTIMATE FASHION STATEMENT

The number and style of a ship's funnels has always been its hallmark. In the early 20th century travellers liked the security and status of a four funnel ship. By the time of Queen Mary, three funnels were the norm.

Each of Queen Mary's funnels was close to a passenger entrance and lift. The middle funnel was for First Class and the front funnel for Third Class.

Queen Elizabeth had only two funnels to give her a more modern look and distinguish her from her elder sister.

Instead of the traditional Cunard red and black, QE2's rakish, thin funnel was controversially painted white in keeping with her bold, modern design. A second funnel to ventilate the kitchen was hidden in her mast. In the 1980s the funnel was repainted red and black to keep traditionalists 'on board'.

Top to bottom Queen Mary (1936), Queen Elizabeth (1940), QE2 (1969).

Opposite Queen Elizabeth celebrated her first Christmas at sea in 2010 with a visit from Santa Claus who came down the funnel.

On her funnel Queen Mary 2 carries one of her namesake's whistles, the tone of whose deep bass A can be heard ten miles away.

On 1st April 2010 passengers aboard the Queen Victoria were surprised to learn from their Daily Programme that while they were on shore excursions the colour of the ship's funnel was to be changed to Britannia Orange. On his return one passenger even complained to the Purser's Office that he did not like the new shade. The date gave the game away.

I NAME THIS QUEEN

Q?

Queen Mary was not the first Queen Mary. That honour went to a Clyde paddle steamer which was built in 1933. Cunard bought the title from the owners, the paddle steamer being re-christened Queen Mary II. Cunard then sought the approval of the Palace to name the liner after the wife of King George V.

The legend persists that the Queen was named thanks to a misunderstanding with the King. A Cunard director approached him for permission to name the ship after 'the most illustrious and remarkable woman who has ever been Queen of England'. He was thinking of Queen Victoria. The King replied 'That is the greatest compliment that has ever been paid to my wife.'

No question

Naming Queen Elizabeth was straightforward. She took the name of the wife of King George VI.

II or 2

Even QE2's name proved controversial. Cunard's strict embargo did not stop the public from speculating or the bookies from offering odds. Shakespeare, Great Britain, Winston Churchill? There was even a suggestion that she would be called Queen Mary 2.

When the Queen named her 'Queen Elizabeth the Second', Scots protested as historically the Queen is the first Queen Elizabeth of Scotland.

Cunard worried about using the Queen's royal Roman II in advertising. The solution was to use Arabic rather than Roman numerals, referring to the fact that she was the second ship of that name. She soon became known simply as QE2.

Left The Queen Mary paddle steamer moored at Victoria Embankment, London, 2009. Her use as an entertainment centre continues after being moved to La Rochelle in France.

PRINCE OF WALES	6/4
PRINCE CHARLES	2/1
MAURETANIA	1/2
JOHN F KENNEDY	7/2
SIR WINSTON CHURCHILL	4/1
QUEEN VICTORIA	5/1
10/1 ANY OTHER NAME	

QE2 + Queen Mary 2

After QE2 it was logical for Cunard to name its next liner Queen Mary 2: both Marys were the largest ships of their day. The ship's illuminated name is 22 metres long and 2.4 metres high.

A real Queen?

Shipyard workers were convinced that 534, the future Queen Mary, was going to be Queen Victoria. In fact the monarch had to wait 70 years to be honoured. Even then some ships' buffs were 'not amused' arguing that, as neither mail ship nor true Atlantic liner, Queen Victoria was an imposter.

A true Ma'am

In 2007, before announcing the order, Cunard sought and won the approval of Queen Elizabeth II to call the ship Queen Elizabeth.

Left Queen Mary 2 illuminating New York.

A TOE IN THE OCEAN

Queen Mary

The tradition of royal christenings began with Queen Mary naming Queen Mary, watched by a crowd of over 200,000 despite the pouring rain. The Queen was clearly nervous. As she stepped forward she whispered to the King: 'Which buttons do I press?' As the liner slipped into the Clyde, the Queen turned to her husband and asked 'Was that right?'.

Right The crest from the cover of Queen Mary launch booklet.

LAUNCH OF
the
" QUEEN MARY "
in the presence of Their Majesties
THE KING & QUEEN
Wednesday, September 26, 1934
at Clydebank

Cunard White Star
Launch of the
 "Queen Elizabeth"
in the presence of Their Majesties
The King & Queen
at the yard of
John Brown & Co. Ltd.
Clydebank
Tuesday, September 27·1938

Naming Ceremony performed by
Her Majesty Queen Elizabeth

26th September, 1938.

The following official statement was issued from Buckingham Palace:—

"At the request of the Prime Minister the King has cancelled his journey to
Clydebank to-night. The Queen, accompanied by Princess Elizabeth and Princess
Margaret, will carry out the programme as arranged. . . ."

The King graciously sent a message by Her Majesty the Queen. The full text of the
Queen's speech appears overleaf.

Queen Elizabeth

The launch of Queen Elizabeth on 27th September, 1938 was a rather more muted affair as King George VI had to cancel because of the Munich crisis, amidst growing concerns that Hitler was to invade Czechoslovakia. The Queen was joined by the Princesses Elizabeth and Margaret. The Managing Director of John Brown's shipyard had to cut the Queen's speech short when the vessel started to move down the slipway: 'Ma'am she's going. Launch her please.'

Opposite The opening page from Queen Elizabeth Launch Book, with an official statement from Buckingham Palace regarding the cancellation of the King's presence at the launch.

Right Embroidered 'Address of Welcome' presented by Cunard chairman Percy Bates prior to the ship's launch.

Below The Queen Mother accompanied by Queen Elizabeth at the launch of Queen Elizabeth.

Queen Elizabeth 2

When the Queen launched Queen Elizabeth 2 on 20th September, 1967, she used the same pair of gold scissors as her mother and grandmother had when cutting the ribbons for the first two Queens.

The Managing Director of John Brown's shipyard vetoed Cunard's suggestion of approaching the Beatles to write and perform a song for the occasion. Instead he invited a local pipe band to play 'Scotland the Brave'.

Queen Mary 2

The Queen named the ship on 8th January, 2004. The crowd of 2000 invited guests included Deputy Prime Minister John Prescott, who started his career as a steward on Cunard liners. The ship was granted the prestigious prefix RMS to honour the tradition that Cunarders carried the Royal Mail.

Queen Victoria

After touring the ship with her husband Prince Charles, Camilla, Duchess of Cornwall, performed the naming ceremony on 10th December, 2007. The bottle of champagne, however, failed to break. So far the ship has escaped the curse that, according to seafarers' lore, follows a ship if the bottle fails to break.

Queen Elizabeth

On 11th October, 2010 the Queen took on the mantle of her mother 72 years before, amid a shower of fireworks and ticker tape. Before the naming ceremony she toured her ship testing out the horn and admiring her portrait. Tickets for the maiden voyage to the Canaries sold out in 30 minutes.

Opposite, clockwise from top left Queen Elizabeth attended four out of the six launches: Queen Elizabeth, Queen Elizabeth 2, Queen Mary 2, and the modern Queen Elizabeth.

Above right Prince Charles and Camilla, Duchess of Cornwall, at the naming ceremony of Queen Victoria.

Madrina

A Queen's first toe in the water is now marked in a very different way. Adopting a tradition dating back to ancient classical times, commemorative coins have been welded beneath the mast for good luck during the float-out ceremony.

A madrina, the ship's godmother, blesses the ship. Queen Victoria's madrina is Maureen Ryan, the only person to have served on four Queens while Queen Elizabeth's madrina is Florence Farmer, whose husband was chief engineer on both the previous Queen Elizabeths.

Above The directors of the Fincantieri shipyard outside Venice presented Queen Victoria's madrina Maureen Ryan with this cork as a memento of a great occasion.

Opposite A bottle of Rothschild white wine is smashed against the hull of the new Queen Elizabeth.

What was in the bottle?

Only two Queens had a champagne send-off.
The nationality of the shipyard influenced the
choice of wine. Australian wine was selected
for the first Queens as a symbol of the British
Empire and Commonwealth. The French and
Italian shipyards opted for champagne, although
Queen Victoria first met the sea bathed in
prosecco. Cunard Line baptised Queen Elizabeth
in its own label of Rothschild white wine.

Queen Mary	Australian sparkling white wine
Queen Elizabeth	Australian sparkling white wine
Queen Elizabeth 2	Australian sparkling white wine
Queen Mary 2	Veuve Cliquot champagne
Queen Victoria	Veuve Cliquot champagne
Queen Elizabeth	Rothschild Cunard Graves white wine

Travel

'Old-style European service,
dinner in formal dress,
dances and games and sports.
Dining is a ritual with rare foods,
fine wines and faultless service.'

Passenger on Queen Mary, 1961

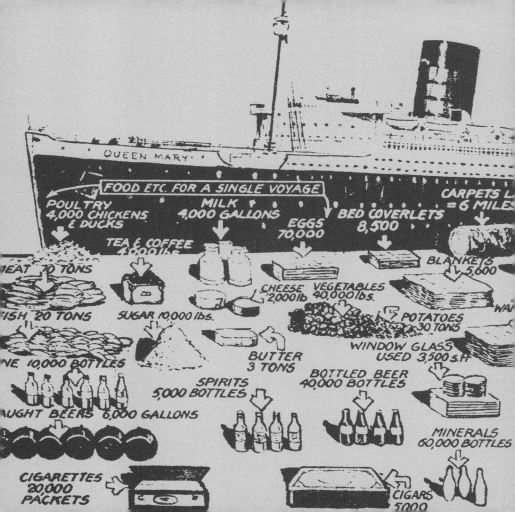

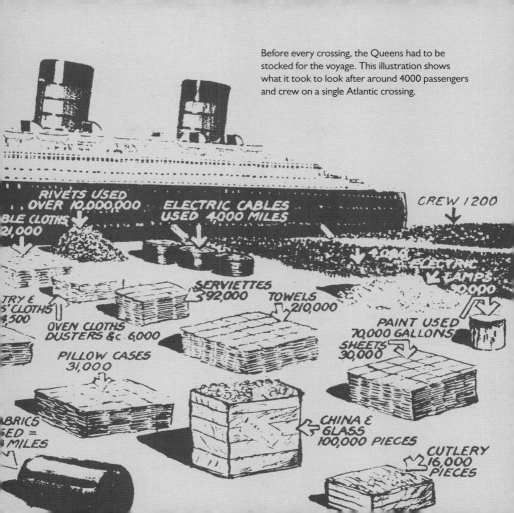

Before every crossing, the Queens had to be stocked for the voyage. This illustration shows what it took to look after around 4000 passengers and crew on a single Atlantic crossing.

RIVETS USED OVER 10,000,000

ELECTRIC CABLES USED 4,000 MILES

CREW 1200

BLE CLOTHS 21,000

TRY & S'CLOTHS 4,500

SERVIETTES 92,000

TOWELS 210,000

ELECTRIC LAMPS 30,000

OVEN CLOTHS DUSTERS &c 6,000

PAINT USED 70,000 GALLONS

PILLOW CASES 31,000

SHEETS 30,000

ABRICS SED = MILES

CHINA & GLASS 100,000 PIECES

CUTLERY 16,000 PIECES

'THE BEST FOOD IN THE WORLD'

From the clink of ice against cocktail glass to the romantic midnight supper, dining has always been a highlight of the Cunard experience. On the first Queen Mary dining was strictly segregated by class, whereas on the second, there are 17 restaurants and bars to choose from.

Not on the menu

As a head waiter on Queen Mary explained: 'If passengers wanted caviar for breakfast they got it.' In First Class Cunard's policy was 'Eat what you fancy' even if the dish was not on the menu. In the 1950s, a US tycoon tested the policy to the limit by asking for rattlesnake steak. Two stewards waving rattles served him eels on a silver platter.

Cheese slices and steak and kidney pie

Cunard checked passenger lists before stocking up for the voyage. When Mr Kraft travelled on the Queens in the 1950s, his cheeses featured on the menu.

Celebrities made their own demands of the kitchen. Actress and singer Frances Day brought her own hens to ensure that her eggs were fresh.

Film star Elizabeth Taylor ordered special meals from the fish chef, not for herself but for her pet dogs. Her own favourite dish was steak and kidney pie while Noel Coward often ordered bangers and mash.

Film star Victor Mature had a gargantuan appetite. He would demolish a 12 lb turkey at a sitting. He always sent his compliments to the chef by autographing the menu with remarks like 'Cunard cooking is as great as sex - almost.'

'Sick all day'

Menus had to be adapted to the weather. In a storm, passengers who could face food at all demanded light plain dishes like bouillon or boiled vegetables rather than roast beef or sponge pudding.

Washed down by...

- 6000 gallons of draught beer and 40,000 bottles of beer per voyage on Queen Mary.

- 43 cocktails on QE2 including 'QE2', a mixture of brandy, orange juice, grenadine, curacao and vermouth.

- Unlimited champagne on QE2 when turbine trouble left passengers in mid-ocean without water in 1974.

- 343 different labels of wine on Queen Mary 2.

- Cunard Rothschild red and white wine on Queen Elizabeth.

Below Queen Mary's chef inspecting a batch of penguin eggs from South Africa.

For starters

Cunard menu covers have become collectors' items. Each meal of a crossing had a different menu cover. Cunard commissioned artists and designers to come up with different themes, from historical anniversaries to impressions of ports of call.

The ship's print shop printed the menu in consultation with the kitchen using packages of pre-printed covers, each marked with the day on which it was to be used.

Below and opposite A selection of exotic menu covers from various voyages taken by QE2.

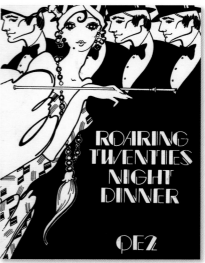

Karachi

KOREA

QUEEN ELIZABETH 2

Sri Lanka
QUEEN ELIZABETH 2

QUEEN ELIZABETH 2 SOUTH AFRICA

SEYCHELLES
QUEEN ELIZABETH 2

MOMBASA
QUEEN ELIZABETH 2

CROSSING THE
Equator
QUEEN ELIZABETH 2

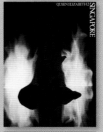

QUEEN ELIZABETH 2 SINGAPORE

QUEEN ELIZABETH 2 BOMBAY

Hong Kong
QUEEN ELIZABETH 2

Caribbean
QUEEN ELIZABETH 2

THAILAND
รายการอาหาร
QUEEN ELIZABETH 2

'LOOKING AS GORGEOUS AS YOUR SHIP'

Dressing for dinner was de rigueur in first class by the 1930s. Etiquette writers warned wealthy Americans not to over-dress: 'It simply isn't considered smart to appear too opulent. It subjects one to the suspicion of having nowhere else to wear one's clothes.'

A tuxedo was essential for men. 'Without it you will have no dances and no Great Moments with the young thing in crepe marocain on the lee of the starboard ventilator.'

Cunard's interior designers chose colours and lighting that would show off passengers' finery to best effect. Even the stewards were impressed. 'I was able to study at close range the 1939 Glitterati in all their Art Deco era glory and finery.

Elegant women in their long gowns with Mink and Fox draped over their pale English shoulders.

A preponderance of long cigarette holders with smouldering De Reske or Turkish cigarettes proffered from gold and silver cigarette cases by portly well fed gentlemen in formal wear, themselves puffing on expensive Havana cigars.'

When crossing, QE2 retained a formal dress code on four out of six evenings. One wealthy American took two top-class suites when cruising, one for herself and one for her clothes. On a 1977, 90 day world cruise, she packed several dresses for each day.

Left Passengers on Queen Mary dolled up for dinner.

Opposite A couple on the deck of Queen Mary dressed for the evening.

FURS *of* QUALITY—

From Barkers at Summer Stocking Prices!

● **Visit** the **FUR SALON, SECOND FLOOR**—one of the cool lofty Salons of the new West Wing, where you'll find shopping both pleasant and untiring, even on the warmest day. Scientific air conditioning **sees to** that!

NATURAL WESTERN MUSQUASH COATS AND SWAGGERS— *at values that cannot be equalled!* Every garment is furriered from perfectly matched . . . reliable . . . full quality pelts. Many styles to choose from!

Illustrated— **A Full Length Coat** with popular adaptable collar, which can be worn closed snugly at the throat in severe weather.

SW fitting.

50 Luxurious
SCOTCH MOLESKIN SWAGGER COATS

Generously cut on tailored lines, made

10

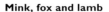

Mink, fox and lamb

Fur was more than a fashion statement on the first Queens. The only central heating on the wintry Atlantic was hot air blown through the ship's ventilators.

Fur was also a precious commodity carried on express liners because of its high value. On a typical crossing in 1951, Queen Elizabeth's cargo list included three bales of raw furs, one bale of raw Australian possum skins and three bales of raw skunk skins.

Opposite An advertisement for fur coats in 'The Daily Mail', c1940.

Left and below Passengers and celebrities such as Hollywood vamp Marlene Dietrich (bottom row, third from the left) dressed for the weather fashioning the popular fur coats on board Queen Mary.

REGENT STREET AT SEA

Queen Mary was the first liner to have a shopping mall. With its 24 large display windows 'Regent Street' included a cigar store, Garrard's the royal jewellers and W H Smith for books and stationery.

Two branches of Austin Reed's reassured passengers: 'Some of the terrors of packing are eliminated by the knowledge that they are not necessarily doomed to a life of seclusion on board if they have omitted some vital article of clothing from their trunks.'

A fountain, deep sofas and baskets of fresh flowers put passengers in the mood to spend.

With cruising, passengers have even more time to shop. Queen Mary 2's Mayfair boutiques include H Stern, Hermes and Harrods, which opened its first seagoing branch on QE2 in 1985.

Above The Duke and Duchess of Windsor were regular shoppers at Austin Reed's Queen Mary branch.
Opposite W H Smith & Son store on board Queen Mary.
Below Hunt & Winterbotham store on board Queen Mary.

Shopping Aboard The Queen Elizabeth 2

Annually, between 80,000 and 100,000 affluent and relaxed passengers will spend up to £4,000 a day in the largest and most elegant shopping arcades afloat: those on the *QE2*. In addition, 49 showcases, specially sited in areas to draw the passengers' attention, will display the products and services of the best British, European, and American companies. These manufacturers and specialist companies see the *QE2* as a magnificent and unrivalled opportunity to present the pick of their products. Overleaf are listed some of the presentations on board.

BOAT DECK

BENDICKS (MAYFAIR) LTD, manufacturers of the finest hand-made chocolates in the world, have the pleasure of serving all passengers aboard the *QE2*. They have five of their own retail branches in the West End of London, and their products are sold by most of the top stores throughout the world from Europe to Australia.
Head Office: Winchester, Hants. Tel: Winchester 63175.

GARRARD The Crown Jewellers. The Garrard showcase on board contains many examples of fine English antique silver and a superb range of modern jewellery and watches. Each item has been carefully selected from the ever changing collection to be found in Europe's most magnificent jewellery showroom. Visitors from home and overseas are always extended a warm welcome.
112 Regent Street, London, W1A 2JJ. Tel: 01 734 7020.

PARFUMS HERMÈS—PARIS
If the Calèche fragrance were a painting, who would have painted it?
Not Gauguin. Not Ingres. Boticelli, perhaps, if his springtime were a French spring, with a little of Monet's softened sunlight dappled in.
If Calèche were a city, what city would you think of?
Avignon. But you might think of Paris, if you took just the right patch of Paris, and set it in the midst of Aix-en-Provence.
And if Calèche were a woman?
If you know, then you must know her from the inside. You'll find a little of yourself in a bottle of Calèche.

UPPER DECK

LENTHÉRIC " 12 ", the classic French fragrance created by the international House of Lenthéric. A rich full-bodied fragrance of haunting fascination, inspired by ideal womanhood as portrayed by twelve of the world's leading artists. Lenthéric " 12 " can be purchased in top department stores and is available at duty-free prices on board the *QE2*.

H. R. OWEN LTD, the famous luxury motor car dealers, specialising in Rolls-Royce, Bentley, Aston-Martin, Jaguar, Daimler, and Rover, pride themselves in being able to demonstrate any of these fine marques anywhere in the United Kingdom.
They have made arrangements for up-to-date information and literature to be immediately available to passengers on the QE2.
Head office: 17 Berkeley Street, London, W1. Tel: 01 629 9060.

QUARTER DECK

BENSON & HEDGES special filter king size cigarettes—packed in the distinctive gold box which has become famous around the world—are the world's fastest-growing Virginia filter cigarettes. Smooth and satisfying, they are to-day England's largest-selling king size brand—another outstanding British product made available to *QE2* passengers.

LYLE & SCOTT of Hawick are famous throughout the world for their finest Scottish knitwear for men and women. Traditional Scottish skill and impeccable styling are combined with the highest quality cashmere and lambswool in exclusive colours.
London showrooms: Henrietta House, 9 Henrietta Place, London, W1. Tel: 01 636 4904.

MARY QUANT COSMETICS, Chelsea, London. A whole load of no-nonsense goodies for the strictly up-to-the-minute female. From nudely natural make-up, to lipsticks and nail polishes that are colourfully " now ", from breakthrough eye shiners to perfumes and fragrances that don't pull any punches. Stand out with Mary Quant.

ROTHMANS of PALL MALL LIMITED. Rothmans King Size filter cigarettes will be available on board in two specially designed packings: one in the form of a 200's decorated tin and the other in the form of an illustrated card sleeve, both these packings feature the *QE2*.
Rothmans King Size is sold on six continents, in over 160 countries, on more than 100 airlines and on more than 150 shipping lines. It is the World's Largest Selling King Size Virginia cigarette and Britain's most exported one.
Park Lorne, 111 Park Road, London NW8.

VICEROY King-size Filter Cigarettes, on sale to *QE2* passengers, are one of America's best-known brands. Not as strong as some US cigarettes, not as light as others. Viceroy have a balanced American taste which will appeal greatly to British smokers as well as to their American co-passengers.

TWO DECK

BEEFEATER GIN (London Distilled). Acknowledged by connoisseurs of genuine London gin, Beefeater is identifiably excellent in the Beefeater Dry Martini, the most called for brand name among cocktails in the whole world. Beefeater owes its superlative quality and fineness to the Burrough family method of distillation.
James Burrough, Beefeater House, London, SE11.

PARFUMS GIVENCHY. Once the privilege of Audrey Hepburn. Unblushingly sophisticated . . . impishly wise . . . wildly romantic, this is L'Interdit by Givenchy.
As to Le De Givenchy, its sunny floral scent identifies unmistakably its following.
Both perfumes are suited to any day-time activity and will enhance your personality with a fabulous chic that will become yours.

Q IS FOR QUOITS

Deck games on liners arose in the late 19th century as a way of exercising and of passing the time. On Queen Mary the area laid out for deck games was equivalent to Wembley football pitch.

When the emphasis switched to cruising, on board leisure activities mushroomed. By the 1980s Cunard claimed that it would take a passenger four months to experience all QE2's leisure pursuits.

Even today when the Entertainment Director manages a staff of 130, deck tennis remains a favourite on Queen Mary 2.

Some of the more unusual deck games played on the Queens have included:

Bubble-Puppy Also known as spiro-ball, this was essentially tennis for one player.

Deck quoits Players take turns to throw the quoits, hoops made of rope, at a target of circles marked on the deck.

Giant Holo The player had to coax a ball through a tunnel with a stick. The game was played on a boxed-in court to stop the ball ending up in the sea.

Putt-putt In the 1980s an ocean version of a mini-golf course was installed on QE2.

Shuffleboard Introduced in the 1870s, shuffleboard is probably the most popular deck game of all time. Up to four players take turns to slide discs with a cue onto a target area painted on the deck.

+10		
6	1	8
7	5	3
2	9	4
-10		

Left A shuffleboard target.

Opposite Shuffleboard on QE2.

Tennequoits Ocean liners first made this hybrid of tennis and quoits popular. Players toss a small ring back and forth over a net. A favourite shot was the macaroni thrown in such a way that it wobbled unpredictably and was harder to catch.

If passengers tired of deck games, there were competitions – the four-legged race; the wheelbarrow race with a human as the barrow; the biscuit and whistle race where the winner was the first to whistle a tune through a mouthful of dry biscuit. In the Cigarette and Needle race, the man had to thread a needle while his female partner puffed her way through a cigarette.

THAT CAN'T BE...

Celebrity spotting has always been a popular passenger pastime. Some stars positively courted publicity, both from the ship's on board photographers and from the Gangplank Willies, waiting at Pier 90 with their cameras and reporters' notebooks. Other celebrities shunned the public eye, either travelling incognito or rarely leaving their cabins during the voyage.

Shipboard photographers worked in the darkroom overnight to develop snaps of passengers which were displayed on a board outside the dining room next morning.

New York hit moves to London

In the days when by sea was the only way to cross, theatre performers moving from Broadway to the West End, sports teams on their way to a big match, Hollywood stars shooting in Europe and even top race horses travelled on the Queens.

Right A Gangplank Willy interviewing a celebrity passenger.
Below left Comedians Laurel and Hardy.
Below middle Automobile millionaire, Henry Ford II.
Below right Actor and singer, Eddie Cantor.

Fred Perry, three times winner
of Wimbledon and the US
Tennis Championships.

Jesse Owens, 'the fastest man alive' bringing home four Olympic golds on Queen Mary in 1936.

The irony was that a black American should triumph in an Olympics masterminded by Hitler to showcase the prowess of the Aryan race.

USA weightlifting Team, 1959

Palestine/Eretz Israel football team who participated in the 1938 World Cup qualifying matches. This team was the first Arab-Asian team to participate in World Cup qualifiers.

PORTS OF CALL

The fun way to the sun

Although Cunard had invented the world cruise as early as 1922 with 300 millionaires and their servants on board the Laconia, QE2 was the first Queen specifically built to cruise as well as cross.

In old age Queen Mary and Queen Elizabeth had been sent cruising in an attempt to earn much needed dollars.

'The new QE2 will not merely ferry passengers glamorously back and forth across the Atlantic. Instead she will operate as a self-contained, sea-going resort, offering vacationers unmatched facilities for fun and relaxation.'

The 'bold experiment' was a success with the new Queens following QE2's trailblazing path.

While excursionists now personally record every minute of their shore visits, in the late 1930s they had to rely on the on board photographers to capture that dramatic sunset or the friendly 'natives'. These remarkable photographs of cruise destinations of the era come from the Murley Copeland collection: they feature the same locations as the new Queens visit today.

Left Queen Elizabeth Indian Summer Cruise Brochure.

Opposite, left column, top to bottom Cannes, Cape Town and Venice.

Opposite, right column, top to bottom Panama Canal, Bergen and Miami.

Getting there is half the fun

Even in today's era of world cruising, there are few spectacles as dramatic as the first sight of New York.

'Nothing can rob a voyage of its unique excitement. Ahead lie the towers of Manhattan: anticipation of a landfall is a never-failing thrill. It enhances all your present pleasures all the way across the ocean.'

Cunard Magazine, 1955

LACKAWANNA RAILROAD

Main image Passengers on the deck of Queen Mary with a perfect view of New York.

Right Queen Elizabeth Atlantic Cruise Brochures.

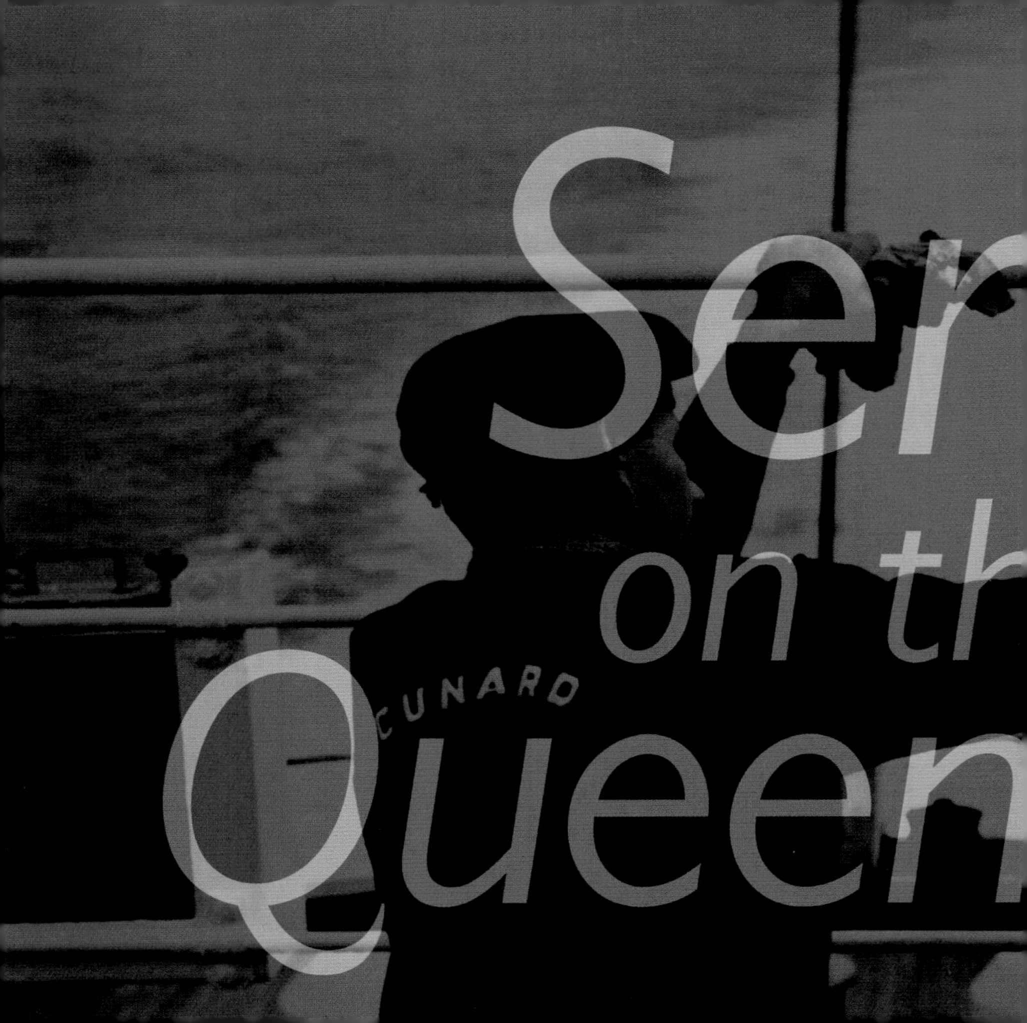
Ser
on th
Queen
CUNARD

ving

'It was with the crew that
Cunard made their name.
It was the personal service
that made the Queens famous.'

Steward, Queen Mary

FAMILY TREE AT SEA

Samuel Cunard chose his captains and crew with care, setting a tradition that Cunard Line honours to this day.

From the start the Queens operated a strict hierarchy on board. Everyone knew their place and from whom they took their orders. Each line of command from deck boy to butcher could be directly traced back to the captain who was in sole command of the ship.

The makeup of the crew has changed over the years. In 1936, 1182 officers and crew signed on for Queen Mary's maiden voyage while the complement for Queen Mary 2 is around 1250.

As crossing became cruising and technology advanced, the ratio of catering and entertainment staff to seafarers increased dramatically. Nationalities also changed. Queen Mary's crew were very largely British, many living around her home port of Southampton. The crew on the new Queen Elizabeth is global.

Jobs now are very different. The 'black squad' of trimmers, firemen and greasers vanished with the end of steam. A rough bunch rarely seen on deck, they fed the first Queens insatiable appetite for coal.

The massage therapist has taken over from the Turkish baths attendant and with greater informality on board, the clothing presser is now redundant. Queen Mary's Lady Assistant Purser who organised parties and games on board is now the Entertainment Director managing a cast of hundreds from guest lecturers to cabaret dancers.

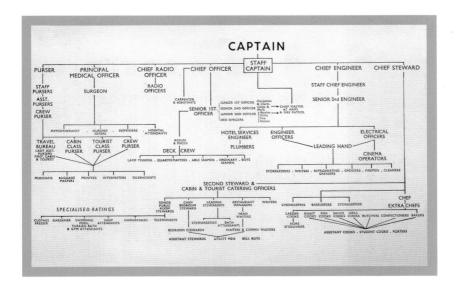

Above Hierarchy diagram from Queen Mary facts and figures brochure, c1950.

Opposite Queen Elizabeth's stewardesses photographed on deck, c1950.

AYE AYE, MADAM

Some remarkable seafarers have captained the Queens. On 1st December, 1935 Commodore Edgar Britten became the first of Queen Mary's 33 captains. He recorded her sea trials, royal visitors, the maiden voyage and six Atlantic crossings in her first log book.

In 1938 Commodore Sir Robert Irving performed one of the great feats of seamanship. During a port strike he docked Queen Mary in New York without the assistance of tugs.

Commodore George Cove took Queen Elizabeth on her maiden voyage and regularly entertained the Duke of Windsor on the bridge.

Commodore Ivor Thompson was a lifelong Liverpool football supporter, his mood on Saturdays being influenced by the score. He was in command when the Queen Mother sailed on Queen Elizabeth to North America and back on Queen Mary in 1954.

Opposite Captain James Bisset, 1947, checking a fact in 'Ship Ahoy: Nautical Notes for Ocean Travellers'. He wrote the book in the 1920s to help passengers understand how a great ship operated at sea.

Right Commodore Edgar Britten and the first log book.

On retirement many captains settled down to write their memoirs. In 1956 Harry Grattidge started his autobiography with the sentence: 'It was the last ten minutes of the last hour afloat.'

When Edward Treasure-Jones, Queen Mary's last captain, was asked why he had not followed this tradition, he replied: 'Who'd read it?'

Commodore Geoffrey Marr took Queen Elizabeth on her final voyage in 1968. He could not settle to life on land and signed on as second mate of a banana boat.

The captain's social duties increased with cruising. In 1980 Captain Robert Arnott recorded in his diary: '365 handshakes with incoming passengers in 34 minutes'.

Watching Queen Mary and Queen Elizabeth sail past his college window gave student Bernard Warner the ambition to command his own Cunarder. He realised it as Master of Queen Mary 2.

Captain Ian McNaught was QE2's youngest and last Master. Some passengers refused to believe that he was the captain as he lacked grey hair and a grizzled beard. He referred to Queen Mary 2 as 'scary Mary' but got to grips with the new pod technology as first Master of Queen Victoria.

In 2010 Cunard Line appointed its first ever female captain to take command of Queen Victoria. Being brought up in the Faroe Islands gave Inger Klein Olsenwould a lifelong love of the sea.

Left to right Commodores Sir Robert Irving and Harry Grattidge, and Captain Robert Arnott.

Commodores William E. and Ronald W. Warwick made history as the only father and son to captain the same Cunarder, QE2. In all they took the helm of the first four Queens.

Above left Commodore William E. Warwick photographed on board Queen Mary.

Above right Commodore Ronald Warwick featured on 'The Illustrated London News' cover, 3rd May, 1969.

'In 1969 QE2 was brand new: no one had ever seen anything like it. As I stood on QE2's bridge with my father, I decided to join Cunard with the ambition of one day becoming captain.'

Commodore Ronald Warwick

STEWARDS SHOULD REMEMBER...

Shipping lines and training schools produced guides on what makes a good steward.

Do:

Find out in advance of serving what snowflake salad or potage Jackson is.

When serving passengers, turn slightly away and retain the breath as much as possible.

Restrain outward expression of annoyance even under the most trying circumstances.

Do not:

Fall asleep in a passenger cabin while cleaning it.

Fraternise with passengers of the opposite sex.

Use a passenger lavatory, however urgent the need.

Right *'Ship Steward's Handbook'*, 1956.

TUMBLER

FRUIT KNIFE
FRUIT FORK

SWEET FORK
SWEET SPOON

SIDE PLATE

MAIN FORK
ENTRÉE FORK
FISH FORK

MAIN KNIFE
ENTRÉE KNIFE
FISH KNIFE
SOUP SPOON
SIDE KNIFE

TABLE NAPKIN
NAPKIN RING

'Stewards should remember always to wipe the bottom of the plate before placing it on the table, and to make sure the food has been placed on the plate to make the dish appear as appetising as possible. If food is placed on the plate tastefully, it helps considerably towards the enjoyment of the meal.'

Dinner lay-up, Officers' Mess, 'Ship Steward's Handbook' of 1956

A day in the life of Geoffrey Le Marquand, commis waiter on Queen Mary, 1957

5am   Rough night. Felt her rolling a lot from my top bunk.

6am   Called on duty by the Gloryhole steward. Only minutes to wash and dress.

7am   'Good morning, Sir'. Held open the starboard doors for early breakfasters.

8am   Helped one of the stewards at table. He's popular with passengers: means that tips are better.

9am   Cleared tables before grabbing a bite myself.

10am Laid tables for lunch in the first class dining room. Mopped the floors again.

11am On duty at the Captain's service handing out hymn books and taking the collection.

12am Quick break and then back on duty at the restaurant doors.

2pm   Same routine – serving lunch, eating lunch.

4pm   While strolling on deck spotted world heavyweight boxing champion Floyd Patterson working out.

5pm   No chance of a chat as my nine cabin mates were snoring.

6pm   Picked up the smoked salmon trolley from the galley.

7pm   Another order to carve smoked salmon at table. Tricky controlling the trolley in this weather.

8pm   Sharpened my carving knife for the umpteenth time – the passengers like it. Tony Curtis at dinner tonight.

9pm   Time to eat – great food too as we get the same as the passengers.

10pm Down to the crew bar the Pig & Whistle, after the breakfast routine for tomorrow.

11pm Lights out and out like a light.

ACCOUNT OF WAGES

Ship and Official Number	Description of Voyage	Ref. No. in Agreement	Condition of Service		
QUEEN MARY 164282	FOREIGN	K41D			
Surname of Seaman	Other Names or Initials	Dis. "A" No.	Rank or Rating		
MARQUAND	G	R654480	A/Stwd		
Port of Engagement	Date Wages Began	Date Wages Ceased	Rate per Month		
	20/3	7/4	30/-		

Above Geoffrey Le Marquand at work and play.

Right Geoffrey Le Marquand adopting the same pose when he visited Queen Mary in Long Beach in 1995, as he had at sea on the same ship in 1957 *(far right)*.

Opposite A pay slip from 1958.

COMING, MADAM

Many young lads dreamed of a life at sea on a Queen. The first step was to become a bellboy. They were at the beck and call of passenger bells all day. They ran errands, delivered telegrams and event programmes, fetched steamer rugs and opened the dining room doors.

It was a hard life for a fourteen year old. Bellboys had to scrub the decks before changing into their uniforms for inspection at 7am. They were subject to the ever watchful eye of the Bell Captain and the Chief Steward.

There were benefits too. Bellboys could earn more than their wage in tips. They met the rich and famous and were allowed to swim in Queen Mary's First Class pool during dinner.

White-gloved bellboys still escort passengers to their staterooms on the Queens.

Right Sir James Bisset inspects the bellboys on Queen Elizabeth.

'A bellboy could go anywhere. You could go from the decks of the ship to the storeroom and right up to the Captain's bridge.'

'They'd inspect your fingernails and things. Make sure your uniform was clean and tidy, shoes polished, haircut, to go on duty that day.'

'It was a twelve hour day. We had twenty minutes off to grab a meal. There was nowhere to sit unless you could find an old orange box somewhere in the crew's quarters.'

'Up in the morning, we used to do gym. Then we'd come down, get changed, go and have breakfast and then get on our uniform.'

DOG DAYS

Walkies!

One of a bellboy's many duties was to walk the dogs. Queen Mary had 26 kennels, each with a removable teak floor, skylight, hot and cold water and central heating. Dog-lover the Duke of Windsor remarked on the lack of a lamp post beside the kennels. Cunard immediately obeyed the royal command. It later installed a lamp post convenience on QE2.

Cunard offered a dog walking service. One Queen Mary bellboy recalled: 'We used to get some terrible little dogs – always fighting each other. You'd have to drag them around the deck for about half an hour and take them to see their owners on the prom deck.'

Not every dog enjoyed the experience. In December, 1935 aviator Charles Lindbergh brought his family to Britain for safety after the sensational trial of his child's kidnapper. The dogs followed on Queen Mary. Lindbergh wrote to his mother 'I am afraid they have not appreciated the honour.'

Cunard Line retains its White Star service for dogs on Queen Mary 2.

Asta the Dog

Asta was a star in his own right. The cute little wire-haired terrier featured in films like 'Bringing Up Baby', 'The Awful Truth' and the popular 'Thin Man' series.

Returning to Hollywood on Queen Mary in 1939, after filming in England, Asta escaped from his exercise yard. A late night search found the dog an hour later curled up asleep in a deck chair.

Left Asta the dog photographed aboard Queen Mary.

Opposite Queen Mary 2 steward walks dog on deck.

RACOONS, RACEHORSES AND RATS

Crew on the Queens have looked after some exotic passengers.

Racehorses crossed the Pond on the first Queens to breed or run in top events. They wore special shoes to stop them slipping on deck. Film star and stuntman Tom Mix fitted one of Queen Mary's life belts round his horse's neck for the benefit of photographers.

Surrealist artist Salvador Dali is supposed to have booked two suites on QE2 in the mid 1970s, one for himself and the other for his two pet cheetahs. The cheetahs destroyed their cabin, and after a brief spell in the kennels, they were evicted. Even modern Queens have a shipboard cat.

A rat for Sunday lunch

Crew have also smuggled pets on board.

A printer on Queen Elizabeth kept a monkey in a bread cage in the Print Shop. When let out for a breather, the monkey leaped into the air conditioning shaft in the ceiling. It hid there for four days. When the ship reached Southampton, it was bribed out with a large bowl of fruit.

During a QE2 cruise to South America in 1980 a crew member smuggled aboard Basil the pet boa constrictor along with a large, live, white rat for Basil's Sunday lunch. With the rat in his mouth, Basil made a break for freedom. Eventually cornered, the culprits were last seen swimming for the shore.

Opposite Colonel Phillips and pet racoon on board Queen Mary.

'She was like a phantom ship steered by phantom hands.'

Robert Stein, Engineer on Queen Elizabeth's maiden voyage

eens

aking

history

QUEEN MEETS QUEEN

The Queens have met on several historic occasions.

The world's three greatest liners (from left to right) Normandie, Queen Mary and Queen Elizabeth in New York, 1940.

Queen Mary 2 meets Queen Mary, Long Beach Harbour, 23rd February, 2006.

Queen Victoria meets Queen Mary, Long Beach Harbour, 3rd March, 2011.

Royal rendezvous between QE2 and Queen Mary 2, Fort Lauderdale, Florida. 10th January, 2007.

Queen Elizabeth meets Queen Mary 2 in Sydney Harbour on 22nd February, 2011 to mark the 70th anniversary of the wartime meeting of troopships Queen Mary and Queen Elizabeth in 1941.

Thirteen is a lucky number

Queen Victoria, Queen Mary 2 and QE2
met in New York Harbour on 13th January, 2011.
Three years to the day Queen Mary 2, Queen
Victoria and Queen Elizabeth celebrated
a second royal rendezvous.

New York knows how to deliver a royal
welcome ever since Queen Mary docked
in 1936 to ticker tape streamers and fireboats
spraying fountains of water.

In 2011 the town was painted red. Commodore
Bernard Warner rang the closing bell of the
New York Stock Exchange. The Empire State
Building glowed Cunard Red. The three Queens
rendezvoused at the Statue of Liberty under
a shower of fireworks before setting off on
their different voyages.

Opposite The three youngest Queens rendezvous under
the Statue of Liberty, 13th January, 2011.

Right The Empire State Building glows Cunard Red,
13th January, 2011.

CROSSING THE LINE

The tradition of marking the crossing of the Equator is supposed to date back to earliest times. A crew member was sacrificed to the ocean to bring good luck and a safe passage to the ship. Naval vessels started the modern ceremony as a rite of passage for new seafarers.

Cruise liners were not the first Queens to cross the line. Both Queen Mary and Queen Elizabeth switched from summer to winter in a second when trooping to Australia.

Today Cunard invites passengers and crew, who have never crossed the Equator before, to become pollywogs. Bearing his trident King Neptune sits with his court at one end of the swimming pool. The ship asks him for permission to cross the line. The pollywogs have to kiss a fish and confess their crimes.

The King metes out punishment which involves the pollywogs being rolled in whatever messy substances, from cooked spaghetti to baked beans that the galley can muster. The pollywogs take a dip and emerge after 'gunking' as shellbacks. A signed certificate from the captain recognizes their new-found status.

Right and opposite Passengers and crew celebrate crossing the Equator in fancy dress aboard Queen Mary.

In 1987 Princess Diana attended a children's party on board QE2. Six years earlier passengers had watched her wedding while mid-Atlantic.

RED CARPETS UP THE GANGWAY

Clockwise from top left In May 1936 King Edward VIII toured Queen Mary in Southampton. By the end of the year he had abdicated. With his wife, the Duchess of Windsor, he was a regular passenger on Queen Mary in the 1950s. Queen Elizabeth, the Queen Mother, was a frequent visitor to her namesake and favourite ship. In 1991 The Duke of Edinburgh and HRH Prince Edward attended a Royal Ball on board in Southampton. Former Prime Minister Margaret Thatcher visited QE2 to commemorate the 10th anniversary of the Falklands Campaign, 1992. Prince Andrew was guest of honour at a lunch to mark QE2's return to service after a major refit in 1994. HRH Princess Anne, the Princess Royal, viewed QE2 from the Royal Yacht Britannia on the 50th anniversary of D-Day, 1994. She made her one and only visit on board QE2 in Edinburgh, July 1995.

TROOPING TO VICTORY

A condition of the Government loan to build the first two Queens in 1934 was the right to requisition them as naval vessels in the event of war. Five years later the Queens were called up.

Queen Mary

When the Second World War broke out, Queen Mary was in mid-Atlantic, with 2332 passengers on board.

With her portholes blacked out and a ban on smoking on deck at night, she made for New York at top speed. She took a zig-zag path to confuse hunting U-boats.

She spent the winter of 1939 at Pier 90, painted in drab battleship grey. On 6th May, 1940, less than three weeks after receiving the order to sail, Queen Mary took on her first troops in Sydney, Australia. Tiers of bunks and hammocks were the order of the day to carry 5500 Anzacs rather than 2140 passengers. In the heat of the Tropics many troops preferred to sleep on deck.

Left Anzacs boarding Queen Mary.
Opposite Queen Mary illustration depicting her wartime voyages.

"Queen Mary"

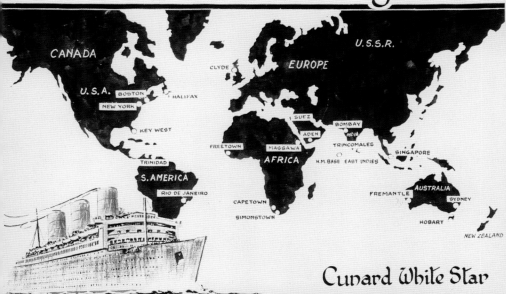

CANADA
U.S.A.
BOSTON
NEW YORK
HALIFAX
KEY WEST
TRINIDAD
S. AMERICA
RIO DE JANEIRO

CLYDE
EUROPE
U.S.S.R.
SUEZ
ADEN
BOMBAY
INDIA
TRINCOMALEE
FREETOWN
MASSAWA
AFRICA
H.M. BASE EAST INDIES
SINGAPORE
FREMANTLE
AUSTRALIA
SYDNEY
CAPETOWN
SIMONSTOWN
HOBART
NEW ZEALAND

Cunard White Star

WARTIME VOYAGES.

New York, Trinidad, Capetown, Fremantle, Sydney.

Sydney, Fremantle, Capetown, Simonstown, Freetown, Clyde.

Clyde, Freetown, Capetown, Simonstown, Trincomalee, Singapore, Sydney.

Sydney, Fremantle, Bombay, Fremantle, Sydney.

Sydney, Fremantle, Trincomalee, Fremantle, Sydney.

Sydney, Singapore, Fremantle, Sydney.

Sydney, Fremantle, Trincomalee, Suez, Trincomalee, Fremantle, Sydney.

Sydney, Hobart, Sydney, Fremantle, Trincomalee, Suez, Trincomalee, Fremantle, Sydney, (2 voyages).

Sydney, Hobart, Sydney, Fremantle, Trincomalee, Suez, Trincomalee.

Trincomalee, Capetown, Trinidad, New York.

New York, Boston, Key West, Rio de Janeiro, Capetown, Fremantle, Sydney.

Sydney, Fremantle, Capetown, Rio de Janeiro, New York.

New York, Clyde.

Clyde, Freetown, Simonstown, Suez, Simonstown, Rio de Janeiro, New York.

New York, Clyde.

Clyde, New York, Clyde, (2 voyages).

Clyde, Boston, New York, Clyde.

Clyde, Freetown, Capetown, Aden, Suez, Massawa, H.M. Base East Indies, Fremantle, Sydney, Fremantle, Capetown, Freetown, Clyde.

Clyde, New York or Halifax, Clyde, (28 voyages).

Queen Elizabeth

On the outbreak of World War II, Queen Elizabeth was little more than a hull with engines, which the 3500 shipyard workers used as an air raid shelter. It was decided to move her to New York for safety.

Such secrecy surrounded her four day dash across the Atlantic that Captain Townley was ordered to open the sealed envelope containing details of his destination only when at sea. On 7th March, 1940 she slipped into the next berth to Queen Mary in New York.

Six months later, after being completed, armed and fitted out as a trooper, Queen Elizabeth sailed from Singapore to join the war effort.

Opposite Preparing Queen Elizabeth for war, 1940.
Above 'The War Illustrated', November, 1941.

Real troopers

The Queens roamed the world's oceans as troopships. From April, 1941 they shuttled 80,000 troops to Suez, returning to Australia with shiploads of prisoners of war. Heatstroke and vermin were rife. 'Temperatures in cabins rose to 125° F and we were not allowed to open the portholes.'

After America's entry into the War, they switched largely to the Atlantic run, Queen Elizabeth making 64 crossings and Queen Mary 60. In July, 1943 Queen Mary carried the greatest number of people ever carried on a ship - 16,683 - a record unbroken to this day.

On one occasion, with 15,000 troops on board, Queen Mary rolled within two degrees of the point of no return after she encountered a freak 75 ft high wall of water in mid-Atlantic.

By the end of hostilities in 1945, the two Queens had ferried a million troops to global war zones. Winston Churchill believed that, thanks to them, the Battle of the Atlantic had been reduced by a year.

Right The crammed decks on Queen Mary, 1943.

'We trucked up the pier and were conducted into this building. We knew it wasn't really a building but that was the size of the ship. About 15,000 troops got on board. The Queen was crowded.'

Calvin Floren, USAF, Queen Mary, 1943

A PRICE ON THEIR HEADS

Hitler put $250,000 on the head of the Queens and promised the Iron Cross, Germany's highest honour, to any U-boat commander who torpedoed them. The Queens had two defences against submarine wolf packs – speed to outrun them and a zig-zag course to confuse them.

Queen Mary carried this zig-zag clock on the bridge beside a blackboard on which her route was chalked. It could be set to remind officers when the next zig-zag was due. The Admiralty set the pattern, the time varying from ten to 50 minutes. No U-boat ever collected the ransom.

Opposite An artist's impression of the Curacao collision.
Below Zig-zag clock.

Somebody zigged when he should have zagged

On 2nd October, 1942, Queen Mary was on the final lap of an Eastbound crossing, towards Gourock with over 10,000 troops on board. Whilst zig-zagging at a speedy 28.5 knots through the notoriously treacherous U-boat infested waters, Queen Mary collided with the slower HMS Curacao, a light cruiser, which was one of her naval escorts. Within five minutes the Curacao sank and 329 of her 430 crew perished.

During war service both Queens were under instruction never to stop, and given her passenger numbers and the danger from U-boats, Queen Mary had no option but to steam on to her destination where a hole 'as big as a house' was discovered in her bow.

The accident was kept from the public until the end of the War for fear of damaging morale. Following a legal wrangle between the Admiralty and Cunard neither party was blamed outright for the collision.

'We worked all day long'

As war-time leader, Winston Churchill made four crossings on Queen Mary under the name of Colonel Warden.

On 5th May, 1943 he sailed to New York to meet President Roosevelt and set the date for the Allied invasion of Europe.

Below deck were 5000 German prisoners of war. After long hours working, Churchill relaxed by playing bezique. When alerted that a German submarine was likely to cross Queen Mary's path, he glanced up from his cards: 'We are just as likely to ram the sub as it is to see us first.'

On 5th August, 1943 Queen Mary took Churchill to the Quebec conference that planned the detail of D-day. His bathroom became a command centre. He spent hours testing models of the artificial harbours to land troops on the Normandy beaches.

Wearing a brightly patterned dressing gown, he puffed on a cigar as an Admiral stirred the bath water into a choppy sea. A Brigadier then lowered a lilo into the water to study the effect. Rather than make waves Churchill's wife Clemmie used the bath next door.

In 1944 Churchill made a two way trip across the Atlantic. Although the tide of war was turning, he was tired and depressed. On board he learned of the first V2 bomb attack on London.

Left Churchill puffs on his legendary cigar, with wife Clemmie.
Opposite Letter from Winston Churchill to Cunard, paying tribute to the service of the Queens during WW2.

Built for the arts of peace and to link the Old
World with the New, the "QUEENS" challenged the fury of
Hitlerism in the Battle of the Atlantic.   At a speed never
before realized in war, they carried over a million men to
defend the liberties of civilization.   Often whole
divisions at a time were moved by each ship.   Vital
decisions depended upon their ability continuously to elude
the enemy, and without their aid the day of final victory
must unquestionably have been postponed.   To the men who
contributed to the success of our operations in the years
of peril, and to those who brought these two great ships
into existence, the world owes a debt that it will not be
easy to measure.

Winston S. Churchill

'MEN SHOULD NOT VIEW THIS TRIP AS A VACATION'

From 1942 the Queens ferried a million GIs and Canadian troops to Europe. The men were warned: 'The ship will be very crowded… Officers and Men should not view this trip as a vacation: it will be anything but that.'

Many GIs spent their last days on land practising for life at sea. They 'embarked' on enormous wooden mock-ups of the sides of the Queens and 'went below' to identify their quarters. On the ship itself everything was colour coded right down to the lifeboats, each GI being given a coloured ticket for his section.

Every space was put to use from suites and smoking rooms to the first class lounge. Troops often slept in shifts, in standee bunks stacked up to seven high. Vertigo could be as much a problem as seasickness. The worst billets were the indoor swimming pools which were turned into dormitories.

Opposite Queen Mary at war, c1942.

The kitchens operated round the clock; nonetheless the sheer numbers meant that troops were rationed to two meals a day, each with six sittings. During a crossing troops on Queen Elizabeth consumed 8.5 tons of potatoes, 31,000 eggs and three quarters of a ton of sausages.

Rules, broadcast by the captain at the start of a crossing, governed life on board - no lights on deck at night, no rubbish overboard, no dirty latrines, no fraternising with troops in other sections of the ship, no hard drinking and certainly no sex. When service women were on board, sentries patrolled troop quarters to check that the last rule was obeyed.

They also enforced the rule that troops had to carry life jackets at all times by removing an offender's left shoe until he returned to his bunk for his life jacket.

The men spent off-duty hours reading or playing cards. The PABX sold chocolate, Lucky Strikes and Coca Cola. Gum had to be banned because so much ended up stuck to the decks.

'My first memory as a greenhorn soldier was the trip to England aboard Queen Elizabeth. I had seventeen dollars in my pocket before I got involved in a blackjack game, and by the time I realized we were passing the Statue of Liberty leaving the States, I was already flat broke.'

Joseph W. Zorzoli, USAF

Right Top *'Elizabethan News'*, December 1942.

Right Bottom *'Westward Ho - Souvenir Edition'*, Newsletter published by troops on board Queen Elizabeth.

On board newspapers with good news stories about the progress of the War helped to keep up morale. Many soldiers had never seen the sea before, much less experienced the Atlantic in a winter storm with U-boats hunting below and enemy bombers hovering above.

On disembarking at Gourock, the men were dispersed to training camps throughout Britain before crossing the Channel to fight.

The authorities issued them with a guide as to how to treat their British hosts – never criticise the King, never boast that the Yanks won the last war or assume that a woman wearing a medal was awarded it for knitting socks.

Demob happy

In 1946 the Queens were demobbed, after taking troops back to North America to a hero's welcome. The refits at Southampton included a thorough disinfecting and the removal of millions of graffiti carved by the troops.

Gallons of paint restored the Queens to their pre-War livery. Yards of teak decking battered by army boots were replaced and furniture was retrieved from stores in New York and Sydney. The Queens were ready to resume normal life.

Below Hand rail inscribed with troops' names and initials, taken from Queen Mary.

WHERE TO M'S. C.T. JOE?

New Jersey, 78

New Mexico, 6

New York, 218

North Dakota

Ohio, 103

Oregon, 13

Utah, 10

Virginia, 30

Texas, 6

Wash
D.C.,

Nevada
6

Oklahoma,

Vermont, 7

Pennsylvania, 15

Wyoming, 5, Washington,

North Carolina, 31, Wisconsin,

Florida, 29

Delaware, 3

Indiana, 51

abama, 13

Arizona, 4

ansas, 16

ho, 10

va, 36

rgia, 28

ine, 20

Montana, 12

nsas, 20

Nebraska, 20

alifornia, 107

onnecticut, 34

Colorado, 17

llinois, 119

WHERE TO, MRS GI JOE?

Before returning to 'Civvy Street' Queen Mary had one last duty to fulfil. As Queen Elizabeth was being decked out in her regal finery ready for her maiden voyage, her sister shipped 12,886 GI brides and their babies to America and 10,000 to Canada. She made her fastest crossing ever in only three days, twenty two hours and forty minutes.

Opposite Illustration from the war bride's onboard newsletter *'Mrs GI Joe'*, March, 1946.

Below Queen Mary's shop does a roaring trade.

With most eligible bachelors fighting overseas, young British women had been swept off their feet by the GI Joes bearing stockings and sweets, and by the handsome Canadians in their dashing uniforms.

The troops offered romance, excitement and escape from war-ravaged Britain. Despite the disapproval of the US authorities and many parents, within months whirlwind romances turned into weddings before the husbands departed for war.

'These were milk carts in every sense. The first class swimming pool was turned into a temporary diaper-room. The all-pervading smell was of babies and sour milk.'

Joseph Maguire, *Queen Mary's doctor*

Queen Mary was hastily fitted out with nurseries, nappies, cots, washing lines, playpens and toys. The brides gorged on foods unavailable in rationed Britain: the Captain attributed the high rate of stomach upsets to overindulgence rather than seasickness.

For the brides, it was a voyage charged with emotion, a brief pause between the tears of parting and stepping ashore in an unknown land. Some barely knew the husband waiting, or sometimes not waiting for them in New York.

'I want to wish all GI brides good luck. In 500 years' time, people will say with pride, "My people came over on the Queen Mary." You will be an ancestor. If you do your job properly, you will help to make the Americans understand the British and to like us, because they like you.'

Message from Lord Woolton, *wartime Minister of Food, in Queen Mary's magazine*

Left Illustration from the war bride's onboard newsletter *'Mrs GI Joe'*, March, 1946.

Opposite Bundles from Britain, Illustration.

A PRIME TARGET

In 1982 Argentina invaded the Falkland Islands in the South Atlantic and Britain went to war.

QE2 was one of four Cunard vessels called up during the Falklands conflict. She was converted into a troop ship in only eight days. Unescorted and without air cover, she battled with South Atlantic gales to land over 3000 troops. Captain Jackson never saw the islands that he had sailed 8000 miles to protect. As a prime target for bombers, QE2 disembarked the troops 800 miles away off South Georgia.

'As 140lbs of caviar was taken off in Southampton, 18,500 cases of beer came on board.' Chef Bainbridge's usual grocery list for QE2 included quail, caviar, foie gras, smoked pork loins, pheasant, lobster and duck. For the troops his kitchens turned out cream of leek soup, brisket of beef with beans and potatoes, cold meats and salads, apple pie with custard and lashings of tea and coffee. There were no complaints.

QE2 returned as a hospital ship to Southampton and victory. Back came the five grand pianos, half a ton of caviar, 17,000 bottles of wine, a botanical garden of potted plants and the traditional Cunard colours on the funnel as QE2 returned to cruising.

'It was not a voyage that I enjoyed. After all I was going to war. I didn't know whether I was coming back. We had to steer through thousands of icebergs, some 300 feet high and one mile long, through overcast weather, fog and snow. We knew we were in the greatest possible danger. We had no air cover, no escort. I have never known such a harrowing experience. We were a prime target and I am thankful they never found us.'

Captain Peter Jackson, QE2

Opposite QE2 arriving at Southampton with survivors from the sunken warships, HMS Coventry, Antelope and Ardent — 11th June, 1982.

ARTIST AT WAR

On board QE2 was the first official woman war artist at a front line conflict. The Imperial War Museum, London commissioned Linda Kitson to keep a visual diary of events as they unfolded.

IF ANYTHING SHOULD HAPPEN TO ME — THE ONLY IMPORTANT THING ~~IS~~ TO SAVE IS THE PORTFOLIO OF DRAWINGS Please

UNDER COMMISSION TO:—
THE IMPERIAL WAR MUSEUM
LAMBETH ROAD
LONDON SE1   6HZ
ENGLAND   (Tel: 01-735 8922)

DR. NOBLE FRANKLAND CBE DFC
(Director & Curator)

Above Linda Kitson's instructions, in the event of her being killed, were taped to the inside lid of a large tin trunk containing art supplies and drawings.

Right Artillery in the shopping arcade.

'It was hard not to laugh at the sight of artillery mounted among the rather feminine trappings of the shopping arcade.

When, much later, I reminded Lieutenant Colonel Holt, Commanding Officer, 4th Field Regiment, Royal Artillery of his headquarters in the Perfumery Boutique, he primly corrected, "Not at all, we were in Cosmetics and Jewellery".'

'I worked as far back from the operations as I could, far too close for comfort. I used several pads firmly attached to me by a variety of clips at all times. The hurricanes created by the rotor blades were a menace, and anything blowing around was a genuine hazard to aircraft.'

Far Left Sea King helicopter on deck. The aft deck, normally a luxurious swimming pool, became a landing pad.

Left Ladies' dressing room complete with bomb target equipment - 'perhaps the most incongruous military setting on a Cunarder ever'.

DOWAGER QUEENS

The fate of the first three Queens has been less happy than their reigns. In their last days as liners, one newspaper described the first two Queens as 'dowagers on a drunken spree'.

A $3.4m price on Queen Mary's head

By the mid 1960s fewer and fewer passengers remained faithful to the ageing Queen. On 27th September, 1967 Queen Mary sailed into Southampton after her 1001st and final voyage. One of her 1400 passengers travelled incognito – John Brown, Queen Mary's architect. Chrysanthemums and Cherbourg sole graced the captain's table and the band played 'Auld Lang Syne'.

Put up for auction Queen Mary went to the highest bidder, the City of Long Beach, who planned to turn her into a visitor attraction.

Opposite Passengers boarding the London bus also bound for the Long Beach museum.

'The voyage from Hell'

Queen Mary had one extraordinary voyage to come. As a condition of buying her as a museum, Long Beach insisted on a farewell cruise round Cape Horn to her new home. Queen Mary was too large to go through the Panama Canal. Forced to charter her, Cunard warned that the trip would be slow, hot, rough and not up to its exacting standards of service.

'The voyage from Hell' confirmed Cunard's worst forebodings. The promise of non-stop partying, seven ports of call and history in the making proved irresistible to 1040 Americans. The food was indifferent and bread roll battles between passengers and stewards broke out. One sultry Latin American beauty, rumoured to be a prostitute, was put off at Rio. Passengers fought for the ultimate experience, travelling round Cape Horn on top of a London bus.

Two days after her arrival at Long Beach on 9th December, 1967, Queen Mary formally ceased to be a ship and became a building. Many of her fittings were sold. One shrewd investor made $1m by turning them into souvenirs: crested chamber pots made good champagne buckets. Lucille Ball, Frank Sinatra and Dean Martin were among his customers.

Today Queen Mary remains a floating hotel and visitor attraction in Long Beach.

Right Queen Mary's resting place, Long Beach, California.

'This "noble tribute to the imagination of Man" was born out of Depression, christened by royalty, grew up in elegance, did her duty in wartime, matured as hostess to the rich and famous, showed signs of her age as she was overtaken by the aeroplane and now rests in peace as a museum to herself.'

R.I.P Queen Mary

Commodore's Dinner

**FAREWELL CRUISE TO LAS PALMAS AND GIBRALTAR
FRIDAY, NOVEMBER 8 TO FRIDAY, NOVEMBER 15, 1968**

— o —

A Toast to the Queen Elizabeth

As this 7-Day Farewell Cruise draws to a close, we remember the many happy occasions and the many good friends we have known during this ship's 495 voyages.

We invite you to join us in "Saluting the World's Largest Passenger Liner" in wishing her a "Long and Happy Retirement," and in toasting the success of "Queen Elizabeth 2" which enters service in a few weeks time.

Afternoon tea for one

In the 1960s passenger numbers on Queen Elizabeth plummeted to under a hundred on a winter voyage. Queen Elizabeth was sent cruising to bring in income. With QE2 waiting in the wings, Cunard withdrew her from service. Her final voyage was a week-long cruise to the Canary Islands and Gibraltar in mid-November, 1968.

'*With her record for war or peace unsurpassed... meeting her duty to the last, when she retires from the Atlantic at the end of the year, she'll still be the Queen with a new career.*'

Poem iced on cake celebrating the final voyage of Queen Elizabeth, 1968

Left Bagpipes play as Queen Elizabeth sails from New York for the last time.

Opposite Commemorative dinner menu.

'She has earned a Viking's funeral: if there is a Valhalla for ships, she is there.'

Captain Geoffrey Marr

Gone to the highest bidder

Queen Elizabeth briefly became a floating hotel in Port Everglades, Florida. Taiwanese businessman C.Y. Tung then bought her to be converted into a floating University in Hong Kong.

On 9th January, 1972 fires broke out on board. Arson was suspected although the culprit was never caught. By next morning Queen Elizabeth lay on her side in Hong Kong Harbour. Three years later, on Guy Fawkes Day, the once glorious Queen had enough of the arguments about her future: she rolled over and sank. Today, her ashes lie under a runway of Hong Kong International Airport after her hull was ground up as landfill.

Left The ill-fated Queen Elizabeth in Hong Kong Harbour.

Right Queen Elizabeth hits the headlines once again.

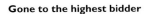

DAILY MIRROR, Thursday, July 20, 1972   PAGE 19

FIREBUGS SET QE ABLAZE IN NINE PLACES

By DONALD W

A SPECIAL squad of marine police and C I D officers has been formed to hunt down firebugs who destroyed the liner Queen Elizabeth in Hong Kong harbour last January.

The 82,998-ton liner, once the pride of Britain's passenger fleet, was engulfed in flames from nine separate points within a few minutes, says an inquiry report published yesterday. The flames spread against the prevailing wind.

And the high speed and immediate spread of ____ fires indicated that they were ____ by unknown

lost between Mr. Tu ardent anti - Comm and his main workers, the five inquiry was told. had been continual squabbles.

Police have few the saboteurs. The team makes no att assign blame—but out accidental "remote" possibili

The grande dame of the seas

By 2008 QE2 was ready to retire. She had sailed over five million miles, the same distance as twelve times to the moon and back. She was the fastest civilian vessel in history: QE2 could travel backwards faster than most cruise ships can sail forwards. It was said that she had undergone more facelifts than Elizabeth Taylor.

QE2 was the most popular Cunarder ever. Demand for her final world cruise was unprecedented as was her 40th anniversary lap of honour round Britain. Her last voyage from Southampton sold out in 36 minutes. Thousands of onlookers shed tears as she called into ports with strong Cunard connections – Newcastle, Liverpool and the Clyde.

QE2 was feted during her last days with royal visits and flypasts. She flew her red 'paying off' pennant, one foot for each year at sea. On 11th November, 2008 the RAF scattered a million poppies over her to mark the 90th anniversary of the Armistice.

That evening QE2 sailed down Southampton Water for the last time.

Opposite QE2 awaiting her fate.

'Queen of the Desert' deserted

Cunard sold QE2 for $100m to the investment arm of the Dubai government as a hotel and entertainment complex. Reassurances were made that she would continue to be treated like a Queen.

QE2 welcomed visitors, Queen Mary 2 and Queen Victoria, with a forlorn toot on her whistle. In 2009 it briefly looked as if she would make yet one more voyage, this time to Cape Town. The deal fell through.

Today QE2 is still laid up in Dubai. One of her nine diesel engines is kept running to power air conditioning, lighting and safety systems while a team of 38 crew carries out essential maintenance.

'For 40 years QE2 has striven to serve her country with flair and fortitude but now her sea days are done and she passes on to a new life in a new home. We wish her well. On behalf of QE2, Southampton I salute you.'

Captain Ian McNaught, at the helm on the final voyage to Dubai

Long live the Qu

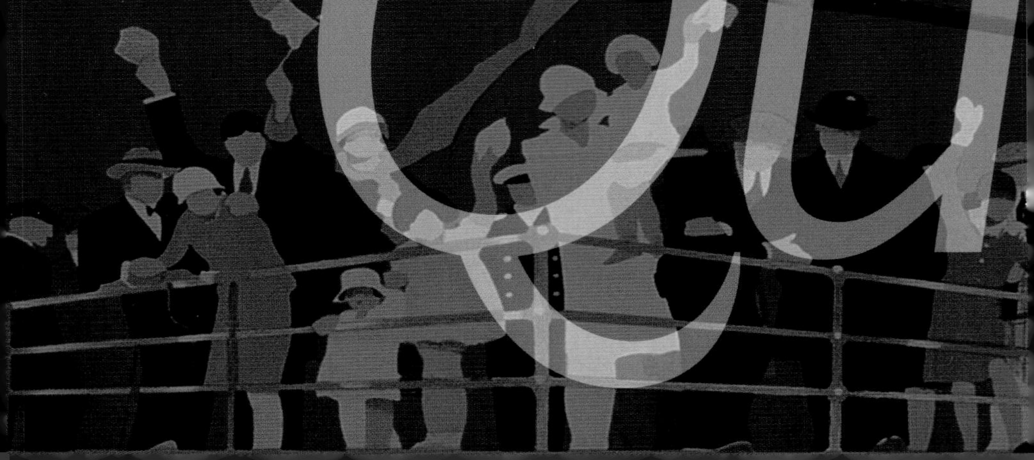

'As a small boy looking at
The Wonder Book of Ships, with
pictures of Queen Mary... I thought:
"one day, I'll go there in command".'

Captain Robin Woodall, QE2

een

PLAYING AT QUEENS

The Queens have become icons of speed, elegance and glamour. Children have played with them and window shoppers have dreamed of them. They have inspired creativity as film sets and settings for novels.

Toys helped children who could only dream of sailing on a real Queen to exercise their imagination. They could take Queen Mary to pieces deck by deck or sail a clockwork Queen Elizabeth across the carpet. Aspiring captains could build their own Queen Mary out of Meccano or Queen Mary 2 out of Lego.

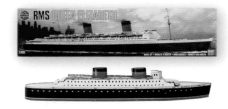

Top right Queen Elizabeth model kit.
Bottom right Queen Mary deck model.

Can you dock Queen Mary?

This docking game recalls a true incident. During a New York port strike in 1953, Captain Donald Sorrell berthed Queen Mary at Pier 90 without the aid of tugs. While performing this remarkable feat of seamanship Sorrell, a small man, stood on a wooden crate for a better view and used a home-made sighting device from nails and a block of wood. Staff from Cunard's New York office acted as stevedores.

Watched by millions on US television, Sorrell succeeded at the second attempt, calmly giving the final order: 'All stop. Finished with engines.' 'Not a lick of paint was lost.'

Leak - Go back to Falmouth

This was just one hazard as players raced their Queen Mary round Great Britain.

Above Queen Mary docking game.
Left Queen Mary board game.

DREAM ON A QUEEN

Cunard sold dreams. It used every trick in the book - advertising, posters, leaflets and even ship models in travel agents' windows.

In the 1930s it promoted 'Your magic steed to Europe' and complained that 'Ships have been boring long enough.' By the 1950s the focus was on pleasure - 'New Ways to Winter Sunshine' and 'Getting there is half the fun'. In the 1960s heritage became part of the proposition - 'Sailing Cunard is a treasured tradition - a passport to exciting pleasures and glowing memories.' Heritage remains integral to Cunard Line's brand today.

Posters from competing shipping lines vied for attention in travel agents' windows. Some featured American icons – the cowboy and the girl posing as the Statue of Liberty. Others promoted the carefree life at sea when cruising.

Above and opposite Posters promoting Cunard Line's transatlantic services on board Queen Mary.

'For all but really experienced ocean travellers, the voyage often begins with the contemplation of posters, examination of photographs and the perusal of booklets by the score.'

'Fodor Guide to Europe', 1938

ONLY THREE TO GO

Children and adults alike collected this series of fifty Churchman's cigarette cards designed to satisfy the public's desire for information about the world's largest liner, Queen Mary (known in the shipyard as job number 534).

STARRING A QUEEN

The Queens have featured on film and television throughout the years. Director William Wyler's **Dodsworth** (1936) about infidelity at sea was partly set on Queen Mary.

She Shall Have Music (1936), a vehicle for bandleader Jack Hylton, tapped into the craze for all things maritime in the year of Queen Mary's maiden voyage.

In **Gentlemen Prefer Blondes** (1953) Marilyn Monroe and Jane Russell play two man-hunting showgirls on a liner. Some sets, first used on Titanic (1953), were adapted to resemble Queen Mary.

Queen Mary was the first liner to feature on Cinerama. **Cinerama Holiday** (1954) showed her sailing into New York at the end of a crossing. Crowds queued outside cinemas on both sides of the Atlantic to marvel at the new wide-screen technology.

Kenneth More and Roland Calver sailed on Queen Elizabeth while filming **Next to No Time** (1959), a comedy set on the ship.

Peter Sellers, Ringo Starr and George Harrison filmed scenes for **The Magic Christian** (1969) on board QE2.

In **SOS Titanic** (1979) the three funnelled Queen Mary stood in for the doomed four funnel liner. Although the director avoided shots showing all the funnels, some scenes showed Queen Mary's Cunard red with black bands livery rather than 'White Star buff'.

Cunarders have also made regular television appearances. Scenes from the classic series **Brideshead Revisited** (1981) were shot on QE2 masquerading as Queen Mary. Passengers had the added excitement of appearing as extras. An episode of **Coronation Street**, Britain's favourite soap, was filmed on board QE2 in 1996.

Since finding her final berth as a museum, Queen Mary has also featured in **Assault on a Queen** (1966), **The Poseidon Adventure** (1972) and **Britannic** (1997). Passengers had the added excitement of appearing as extras.

Left 'Assault on a Queen', film poster, 1966.

Above 'Gentlemen Prefer Blondes', film poster, 1953.

Truth is stranger than fiction

The plot of the disaster movie Juggernaut (1974) was based on a real-life incident on QE2.

On 17th May, 1972, while QE2 was mid-Atlantic, a man telephoned Cunard's New York headquarters threatening to blow up the ship if his $350,000 ransom demand was not met. He claimed that he had planted explosives on six different decks of the ship.

Cunard took the threat very seriously. Crew searched the ship but found nothing. An SAS bomb disposal team of four was parachuted in. The appointed hour passed without incident.

Tailed by the FBI, Cunard Line Vice President Charles Dickson followed complex instructions as to where to leave the ransom. The bag was never picked up and neither bomb nor accomplices were found on board. The hoaxer was eventually sentenced to 20 years in jail.

Right 'Juggernaut', film poster, 1974.

Shipyard Sally

In 1939 singer and actress Gracie Fields made Shipyard Sally based on the story of the building of Queen Mary. She played an out of work music hall actress who serves unemployed shipyard workers in her father's Clydebank pub. She leads the campaign to restart work on Queen Mary.

In the finale she sings 'Land of Hope and Glory' at the launch of Queen Elizabeth, although her most famous song in the film is Wish Me Luck as You Wave Me Goodbye.

'Wish me luck as you wave me goodbye,
Cheerio, here I go, on my way.
Wish me luck as you wave me goodbye,
Not a tear, but a cheer, make it gay.
Give me a smile I can keep all the while,
In my heart while I'm away.
Till me meet once again, you and I,
Wish me luck as you wave me goodbye.'

'*Wish Me Luck*', Harry Parr-Davies, as performed by Gracie Fields in 'Shipyard Sally', 1939

Above Gracie Fields performing on board Queen Mary, 1937 *(left)*, and photographed in Queen Mary's drawing room *(right)*.

READ ALL ABOUT A QUEEN

While maritime historians and seafarers have written about every aspect of the real-life Queens, novelists have set their fictional plots on their decks.

The Queen Elizabeth Family

'Daddy told Belinda: "I'm glad she's British. No one can beat us at shipbuilding - and here's our grandest ship so far!".' Enid Blyton's children's book was based on her own experience of crossing in 1948.

Murder She Wrote

Bestselling mystery writer and amateur sleuth Jessica Fletcher is invited to travel to London on QE2 as one of seven guest lecturers. On the first night a fellow speaker is found brutally murdered. Jessica has just four days at sea to find the killer.

Gut Symmetries

Alice is a British physicist on her way to a research job in the USA. She crosses on QE2 as a guest lecturer. On board she meets Giovanni, one of the most respected quantum physicists in the world. He is a confirmed Lothario and the two soon begin an affair.

Assault on a Queen

'We carry twelve live torpedoes, Captain ... And those torpedoes WILL BE FIRED - unless you do precisely what we tell you.' Five men and a woman plan the most fantastic crime of the century... 'a crime unparalleled in daring and ingenuity'.

Attack on the Queen

Two brothers, each working for different government agencies, must try to stop terrorists from taking control of QE2 with nine of the most powerful world leaders on board.

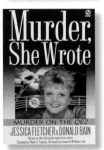

Clockwise from top left 'The Queen Elizabeth Family', Enid Blyton (1951), 'Gut Symmetries', Jeanette Winterson (1997), 'Assault on a Queen', Jack Finney (1960), 'Murder on the QE2', Jessica Fletcher and Donald Bain (1997) and 'Attack on the Queen', Richard P. Henrick (1998).

A pigeon's eye view (from the top of the Empire State Building) of Queen Mary 2 as she sails into New York Harbour for the first time, April 2004